IMPROVING YOUR VO2 IS LIKE FINDING THE FOUNTAIN OF YOUTH

VO2 is a measurement of your body's ability to process oxygen. This is an important measurement of a person's health. It gives a fitness score and determines the amount of calories a person uses when exercising. VO2 goes down as we age but we can counter that decline with cardiovascular exercise. VO2 can be measured directly, which can be expensive and cumbersome, but it can also be measured indirectly very easily by tracking METS. What are METS and why are they important to your health? METS, (Metabolic Equivalent), is an estimate of VO2.

So where do you find your MET level and what is it exactly? A MET is an estimate of oxygen and is represented by a number. Example, 1 MET is the amount of oxygen used at rest, sitting in a chair. That estimate is 3.5 ml/kg/min of oxygen; this is just an estimate, true resting metabolic rates can only be done with metabolic testing. It is still a valuable measure; at 5 METs a person is doing 5 times more work than sitting in a chair. It is simply a measure of work. It can be found on many of the cardio fitness equipment available. People just don't know about it or where to look for it. If you are on a treadmill it is the product of incline and speed, on a bike RPM and gear. It is simply a measure of work. The more work you can do, the higher your VO2, (functional capacity), the more calories you burn for a given time frame of work!

A MET level of 10, (VO2 of 35 ml/kg/min) is considered vigorous activity and should be a goal that individuals could reach or at least touch a 10 MET level as a minimum health goal.

Some estimates of METs are:

Walking 2-4 mph (2-5 METS)

Jogging 6 mph, 1% inclines, (10 METS)

Because METS are a product of work a person can begin to be their own coach and adjust the workload as it works best for them. If you don't want to jog you can adjust the incline higher and stay at a walking pace.

METS are a widely used clinical measure of a person's fitness level and functional capacity. Improving your MET level is said to be finding the fountain of youth! In fact, data suggest for every 1 MET improvement your mortality rate drops by 8 – 17%, and decreases your chance of dying by a heart attack by 10%. Studies suggest that the higher a person's MET level the lower their health care cost tend to be. The key is to track the METS and the higher the number you can achieve the better.

What are your health and fitness goals? How are you going to achieve them? Measuring the metrics that count most is critical to achieving and sustaining your health and fitness goals. Here are some facts to factor into your fitness plan.

- Achieving and maintaining a healthy VO2 is now considered one of the most important health metrics. It can increase your longevity, decrease your chance of heart attack, improve blood lipids, help maintain healthy blood pressure and fight disease.

- Exercise boosts brain function by increasing blood flow and oxygen circulated in the brain. Like your muscles, your brain gets a robust workout during exercise.

- The right exercise will increase the number of mitochondria (powerhouse of the cells). The greater the density in the cell, the greater it's vitality. They are responsible for almost all cellular activity. It is housecleaning for the body! Lean Muscle and body water increase. Because of this increase it is important to check your body composition often, instead of your weight on a traditional scale.

- Cardiovascular exercise helps maintain healthy visceral fat, the fat around your organs, not what wiggles and jiggles. Visceral fat is at the root of inflammation and a host of other medical issues.

- CARDIOZONE is an excellent stress reducer!

While moving is certainly better than not, good health is about more than getting in your steps. You need to pick up both the pace and your heart rate. To have meaningful improvement in your overall health and body composition you need to improve your body's ability to process oxygen. Improving your VO2 is a result of challenging your heart and lungs to do more than you're accustomed. Tracking your heart rate is a valuable tool when you pair it with perceived exertion and workload. When your VO2 improves you will have to do more work than before to achieve the same heart rate. However, you burn more calories in the same amount of time. This will prevent you from having to quit your day job just to be able to burn enough calories to decrease your body fat, especially dangerous visceral fat. In addition as your heart gets stronger it can pump more blood in a single beat. Therefore, when you are at rest your heart doesn't have to work as hard.

There is much evidence that sitting too much is bad for you, no doubt. However, people are being lulled into a false sense of security about achieving good health, that simply getting their steps in will do the trick. Tracking steps with various devices has been and still is all the rage, despite the fact that obesity rates are at an all-time high, and still growing. Simply put, challenging your heart and lungs and improving your workload is key, but what does that look like?

You can dissect heart rate zones a million ways, just look it up on the internet. The important factor is, don't use an outdated age predicted formula. If you are not working with a health and fitness pro to determine your heart rate ranges and Peak VO2, there are still ways you can assess yourself. Note that I used the term Peak VO2 not VO2 Max. Your Peak VO2 is a meaningful measure and is a workload you can achieve multiple times in a workout. VO2 Max is taking you to exhaustion, as in you can't take another step. While there can be diagnostic reasons for this type of assessment, as in a stress test, it is not the picture of what work you can sustain at a given heart rate over a period of time. Using a 3 tier range is an easy way to start tracking your heart rate and workload.

You need to use varying intensity on your workout days with medium intensity as well as interval training days that use all 3 exertion levels. This allows for the improvement of your VO2 and the reaching of your optimal health and fitness goals. They key is to track your workload and heart rate and mix up your exercise intensity. Outside of doing structured workouts, move as much as possible. Take a standing/walking break every hour or two. Take a call standing up and walk around. Your steps are like eating steamed vegetables, it's hard to get too much. However, you still have to get out there and pick up the pace. Varying your activities can prevent boredom and burnout. Core, hiking and yoga can be great zone 1 and often even zone 2 workouts.

Getting outside in Mother Natures gym is great for the body and mind. Most of us spend 90% of their life indoors. Outdoor workouts increase your exertion up to 10%. Zone 3 workouts are often easier to do indoors. However, outdoors is a great place for zone 2, endurance workout or a zone 1 active recovery workout. Science is discovering getting outdoors has significant mental benefits in addition to physical. While being exposed to nature the brain shifts to a positive state. Take your technology with you, strap on a heart rate monitor, get an app with GPS and head out!

The Science of Your Zones

CARDIOZONE® training is cardiovascular training that utilizes *your personal* heart rate training zones, *(determined by our Cardiovascular Assessment)* to maximize your caloric expenditure which improves your health and fitness. Your heart rate zones are used to keep you safe and productive by not over reaching. When training with your proper zones, you increase your body's ability to use oxygen, therefore you burn more calories, improve performance and feel better doing it!

ZONE 1

Comfortable Work. On a perceived exertion scale of 1–10, this is a 5–6. This is an aerobic level effort where you can still speak in sentences doing it. Its a great place to start building a cardiovascular base for those newer to exercise. As your base improves, along with your recovery heart rate, it is appropriate to increase the exercise intensity. ZONE 1 is also used as a warm up and recovery zone. Once the cardiovascular base has been established, ZONE 1 will be referred to as active recovery. It will be used to recover from high intensity interval training after being in ZONE 3. If more than 5 **CARDIOZONE** workouts *(all 3 zones)* are performed in a week, one of them should be a ZONE 1 only workout. If only scheduled for ZONE 1 workouts, do not exceed 6 per week.

ZONE 2

Challenging Work. On a scale of 1–10, this is a 7–8. You can speak but prefer one or two word responses. The top of ZONE 2 is your threshold of burning 100% carbohydrates but not yet working so hard you are anaerobic. You are making lactic acid but keeping up with its production, even putting some back into the energy system. This is your endurance zone and where you will spend most of your training time. Even though fat is not being used as much for fuel, calorie expenditure is up and your heart and lungs are getting stronger. If only scheduled for ZONE 2 *(only Zones 1 & 2)* workouts, do not exceed 6 per week.

ZONE 3

Maximum Work. On a scale of 1–10, this is a 10. This will be a maximum effort for a short time, utilizing anaerobic metabolism. This is your peak training zone which is determined by our Cardiovascular Assessment. Workouts in ZONE 3 use immediately available fuel stored in your muscles and keeps your metabolism elevated for a couple of hours after exercise. While working in ZONE 3 for 1 minute intervals, it is important to make sure you return to ZONE 1 *(just touching ZONE 1)* in the allotted recovery time. If you do not recover in the allotted time, you must wait until you recover to ZONE 1 before continuing the workout. If scheduled for ZONE 3 *(all 3 zones)* workouts, do not exceed 3 per week.

Determine your goal and heart rate zones and get started!

How to Use Your Zones

GOAL: Establishing Cardio Foundation

ZONE 3|2|1 Training 0-1x per week. *(Evaluation required)*
ZONE 2|1 Combo Training 3x per week.
ZONE 1 Training 1-2x per week.

TOTAL = 4-5 Cardio Workouts per week

GOAL: Body Composition Improvement

ZONE 3|2|1 Training 2-3x per week.
ZONE 2|1 Training 2-3x per week.
ZONE 1 Training 1x per week.

TOTAL = 5 Cardio Workouts per week

GOAL: Performance Improvement

ZONE 3|2|1 Training 3x per week.
ZONE 2|1 Training 2x per week.
ZONE 1 Training 1x per week.

TOTAL = 6 Cardio Workouts per week

GOAL: Weight Loss (20lbs+)

ZONE 3|2|1 Training 3x per week.
ZONE 2|1 Training 2x per week.
ZONE 1 Training 1x per week.

TOTAL = 6 Cardio Workouts per week
(Calorie expenditure goal is 3500cal per week)

GOAL: Fitness Maintenance

ZONE 3|2|1 Training 1-3x per week.
ZONE 2|1 Training 1-2x per week.
ZONE 1 Training 1x per week. *(optional)*

TOTAL = 3-4 Cardio Workouts per week

- **ZONE 3|2|1** = Workouts. minimum 45min each
- **ZONE 2|1** = Workouts. minimum 30min each
- **ZONE 1** = Workouts. minimum 45-60min each

ZONES Heart Rates

ZONE 1
Comfortable

Scale 1 2 3 4 **5 6** 7 8 9 10

ZONE 2
Challenging

Scale 1 2 3 4 5 6 **7 8** 9 10

ZONE 3
Maximum

Scale 1 2 3 4 5 6 7 8 9 **10**

ZONES Set Times

Warm Up w/ ZONE 1 10 minutes
Advance to **ZONE 2 5 minutes**
Maximize at **ZONE 3 1 minute**
Recover to ZONE 1 1 minute

Repeat **4-6** Intervals Total

ZONES Interval Workout

Warm Up w/ ZONE1 00:00–10:00
Advance to **ZONE2: 10:01–15:00**
Maximize at **ZONE3: 15:01–16:00**
Recover to ZONE1 16:01–17:00
Advance to **ZONE2: 17:01–22:00**
Maximize at **ZONE3: 22:01–23:00**
Recover to ZONE1 23:01–24:00
Advance to **ZONE2: 24:01–29:00**
Maximize at **ZONE3: 29:01–30:00**
Recover to ZONE1 30:01–31:00
Advance to **ZONE2: 31:01–36:00**
Maximize at **ZONE3: 36:01–37:00**
Recover to ZONE1 37:01–38:00

Track Your METS, CALORIES, VO2 AND FITNESS

I did the math for you. Simply find your weight to the nearest 10lb increment. Get a MET reading from a piece of cardio equipment and track your calorie burn and fitness level.

Weight in LBS			110	120	130	140	150	160	170	180	190	200
Weight in KG	2.2		50	54.5	59.1	63.6	68.2	72.7	77.3	81.8	86.4	90.9
		VO2	CPH	CPH	CPH	CPH	CPH	CPH	CPH	CPH	CPH	CPH
METS	1	3.5	52.5	57.3	62.0	66.8	71.6	76.4	81.1	85.9	90.7	95.5
	2	7	105.0	114.5	124.1	133.6	143.2	152.7	162.3	171.8	181.4	190.9
	3	10.5	157.5	171.8	186.1	200.5	214.8	229.1	243.4	257.7	272.0	286.4
	4	14	210.0	229.1	248.2	267.3	286.4	305.5	324.5	343.6	362.7	381.8
	5	17.5	262.5	286.4	310.2	334.1	358.0	381.8	405.7	429.5	453.4	477.3
	6	21	315.0	343.6	372.3	400.9	429.5	458.2	486.8	515.5	544.1	572.7
	7	24.5	367.5	400.9	434.3	467.7	501.1	534.5	568.0	601.4	634.8	668.2
	8	28	420.0	458.2	496.4	534.5	572.7	610.9	649.1	687.3	725.5	763.6
	9	31.5	472.5	515.5	558.4	601.4	644.3	687.3	730.2	773.2	816.1	859.1
	10	35	525.0	572.7	620.5	668.2	715.9	763.6	811.4	859.1	906.8	954.5
	11	38.5	577.5	630.0	682.5	735.0	787.5	840.0	892.5	945.0	997.5	1050.0
	12	42	630.0	687.3	744.5	801.8	859.1	916.4	973.6	1030.9	1088.2	1145.5
	13	45.5	682.5	744.5	806.6	868.6	930.7	992.7	1054.8	1116.8	1178.9	1240.9
	14	49	735.0	801.8	868.6	935.5	1002.3	1069.1	1135.9	1202.7	1269.5	1336.4
	15	52.5	787.5	859.1	930.7	1002.3	1073.9	1145.5	1217.0	1288.6	1360.2	1431.8
	16	56	840.0	916.4	992.7	1069.1	1145.5	1221.8	1298.2	1374.5	1450.9	1527.3
	17	59.5	892.5	973.6	1054.8	1135.9	1217.0	1298.2	1379.3	1460.5	1541.6	1622.7
	18	63	945.0	1030.9	1116.8	1202.7	1288.6	1374.5	1460.5	1546.4	1632.3	1718.2
	19	66.5	997.5	1088.2	1178.9	1269.5	1360.2	1450.9	1541.6	1632.3	1723.0	1813.6
	20	70	1050.0	1145.5	1240.9	1336.4	1431.8	1527.3	1622.7	1718.2	1813.6	1909.1
	21	73.5	1102.5	1202.7	1303.0	1403.2	1503.4	1603.6	1703.9	1804.1	1904.3	2004.5

Fitness Level	VO2	METS
Building a base	<25	<7.0
Average	25-35	7.0-10.0
Good	36-48	10.3-13.7
High	49-59	14-17
Athlete	60+	18+

Pound to KG = Pounds divided by 2.2
1 MET = 3.5ml of oxygen/KG/Minute
ml to Liter = Divide by 1,000
Calories = 5 calories per liter of oxygen

Interval Training has been established to improve an individual's fitness level (VO2). It increases the amount of calories you burn during and after exercise, as it increases your metabolism. If you determine your MET level is below 7 you are in the building base stage. You can still do modified intervals utilizing zone 1 and zone 2. As your fitness improves to average you can add in zone 3. Below is an example of a CARDIOZONE® interval workout. Always allow yourself time to achieve zone 1 with a 10 minute warmup. If you heart rate has not recovered to zone 1 within 1 minute of doing zone 3, wait until it does. You just borrow some time from zone 2 in your next interval.

THERE'S AN APP FOR THAT

You can't manage it if you don't measure it! Bluetooth Smart technology and various hardware like traditional heart rate chest straps, earbuds and even smart clothing is making it possible for an individual to track their workouts, heart rate, workload, calorie burn and more with the use of various apps right on their phone or smartwatch. One of my favorite apps for tracking workouts is iCardio. This app allows you to monitor a multitude of various activities and keep all the data on one app. You can easily share your workouts directly from the app. iCardio works with both Apple and Android phones. It syncs with Apple HealthKit and various nutrition apps as well allowing your fitness and health information to be stored in one dashboard. There are many apps to choose from; the important thing is to monitor and track your workouts.

CARDIOZONE™ Heart Rates

ZONE 1:
Comfortable

Scale: 1·2·3·4·**5·6**·7·8·9·10

ZONE 2:
Challenging

Scale: 1·2·3·4·5·6·**7·8**·9·10

ZONE 3:
Maximum

Scale: 1·2·3·4·5·6·7·8·9·**10**

ZONE3 WORKOUT Example

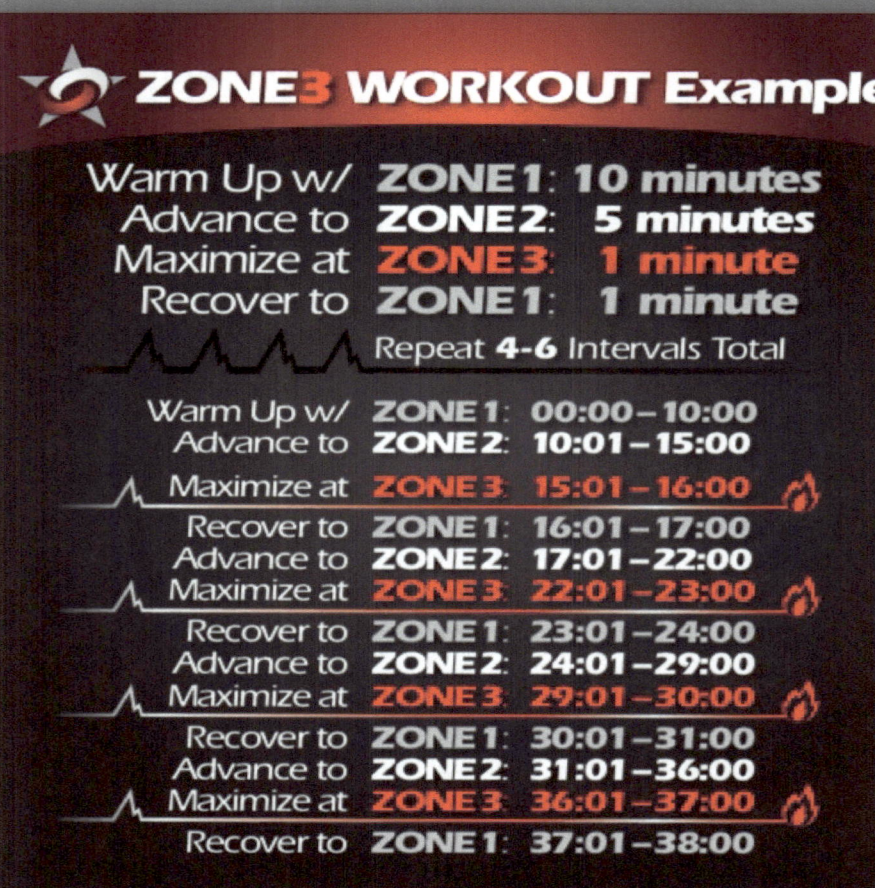

Warm Up w/	ZONE 1:	10 minutes
Advance to	ZONE 2:	5 minutes
Maximize at	ZONE 3:	1 minute
Recover to	ZONE 1:	1 minute

Repeat **4-6** Intervals Total

Warm Up w/	ZONE 1:	00:00 – 10:00
Advance to	ZONE 2:	10:01 – 15:00
Maximize at	ZONE 3:	15:01 – 16:00
Recover to	ZONE 1:	16:01 – 17:00
Advance to	ZONE 2:	17:01 – 22:00
Maximize at	ZONE 3:	22:01 – 23:00
Recover to	ZONE 1:	23:01 – 24:00
Advance to	ZONE 2:	24:01 – 29:00
Maximize at	ZONE 3:	29:01 – 30:00
Recover to	ZONE 1:	30:01 – 31:00
Advance to	ZONE 2:	31:01 – 36:00
Maximize at	ZONE 3:	36:01 – 37:00
Recover to	ZONE 1:	37:01 – 38:00

Standard weight scales don't tell the story of a person's health and fitness levels. BMI, while still widely used is an outdated measure that can paint inaccurate conclusions. Body Composition Scales have improved technology and the professional versions can be very accurate, quick and non-invasive. There are some great consumer models that are comparable to professional scales. The key is getting a model that allows you to choose athletic or active exercise mode. If you are exercising regularly you need to choose active mode or it will over-estimate your body fat. Many models available give important information about a person, in addition to weight and body fat%, such as body water %, visceral fat and muscle mass. There is an unhealthy love/hate relationship that many have with the basic weight scale and what they perceive to be "ideal" weight standards which society has placed upon them.

To explain my point further I will share two scenarios that are representative of what I see in my business on a much too regular basis.

Scenario 1

A middle aged male client, who wants to lose weight, especially in his mid-section, which he says has slowly crept up over the last few years. He has been told, as so many have by their doctors, that he needs to lose some weight. He finds his way to me and I do a complete metabolic assessment and body composition evaluation on him and create his diet and exercise program. He has been weighing himself daily, often multiple times per day, and reports he prefers his morning weight as it is always lower than his afternoon weight. I explain that is because he is coming off a fast as he wakes and the difference is most likely just body water %, because he is somewhat dehydrated upon waking. We make a deal that he won't weigh daily. He will check it weekly but the important thing is I will be monitoring him with the body composition scale so we can track progress. This way he can see what variables actually make up the weight number he sees on the scale. The assessment does determine that his body fat percent is too high and he is carrying too much visceral fat, which is a real health risk. His body water % is a little lower than ideal and he has been on a very caloric restrictive diet with the weight he has lost being composed of water and muscle mass.

The plan is for my client to eat a balanced diet, within the caloric range based upon the assessment I did. We go into that in detail. I set him up with a heart rate monitor and exercise program. These are designed to help him increase the number of mitochondria (power house of the cell) in his body. I explain this is an important health goal. The plan is also going to get his body water up and increase his muscle mass, which are also important health goals. I also explain his traditional scale won't accurately assess this. I let him know that even if the weight number itself doesn't change as much as hoped, as long as he stays to plan important changes will be occurring. I encourage him to judge how he looks when he gets out of the shower, along with how his clothes are fitting, as a much better gauge than what his bathroom scale reads.

Several weeks later, as we meet for a re-assessment, he reports feeling good overall and that his pants are loser in the waist and he has had to tighten his belt! He is excited for me to check his body comp, hoping for change, because his scale is not moving as much as hoped. He gets great results! He has had a decrease in visceral fat, an increase in body water and an increase in muscle mass. We are on the right track and making progress. That is motivating! He reports that he is going in for a recheck with the doctor the next day and looking forward to it. He gets on the traditional scale at the doctors and his BMI and weight have barely changed. His doctor reports this to him as bad news. Luckily, in this case he was packing his body comp results which I encouraged him to take with him. I had already explained BMI to him and why the scale is not a good measure. He was happy, and continued on his journey to drop another 2 % off his body fat percentage, with the majority coming from visceral fat. He reached his goal and is still maintaining it two years later!

Scenario 2

A female client that has a busy work schedule and two children, one toddler and one preschool age. She is frustrated with not being able to lose baby fat weight, and in fact has actually gained a few pounds since her youngest was born. She has tried it all; weight loss programs, pre-packaged meals, working out with various programs, personal trainers, and medical weight loss programs. Yet, she continues her constant battle with the scale. Once again I did a complete assessment and created a customized exercise and nutrition plan for her.

Soon after, peer pressure had her once again obsessed with her scale, caloric restriction and over exercising. She admits that when chatting with friends, or at the gym, they ask her how much weight she has lost with her new program? She responds that she has lost some, but that the scale number is not important as being healthy. Then she reports stripping down to nothing, hitting the sauna and getting on the scale naked, just to get as low of a weight reading as possible. Luckily, she confided with me and we were able to not only re-educate her but motivate her to reach and maintain her goal!

Our knowledge of what defines health has never been greater than it is right now, yet we have never been sicker. Chronic diseases are the leading cause of death and disability in the United States. Chronic disease such as heart disease, cancer, stroke and type 2 diabetes are among the costliest and preventable of all health problems. In the United States, chronic disease, conditions and the health risk behaviors that cause them account for most of the health care cost. Heart Disease is the leading cause of death in men and women. 1 in 4 deaths in the US is caused by heart disease. Improving your body's ability to process oxygen, a measure of your cardiovascular fitness, dramatically decreases the chance of dying by heart disease.

Furthermore, an increase in energy expenditure from physical activity of 1000 kcal (4200kJ) per week or an increase in physical fitness of **1 MET (metabolic equivalent)** was associated with a mortality benefit of about 20%. This is important information in the preventive health front, from medical to commercial fitness. This should be taught to the general population, just like tracking their blood pressure, cholesterol and weight. An increase in physical fitness will reduce the risk of premature death, and a decrease in physical fitness will increase the risk. The effect appears to be graded, such that even small improvements in physical fitness are associated with a significant reduction in risk.

The largest study to date, on the impact of fitness level on mortality rate, was conducted by the Cooper Clinic, in Dallas Texas. The study was comprised of 13,344 participants (10,224 men, and 3,120 women). The participants all received a preventive medical examination and their physical fitness was measured by a maximal treadmill exercise test. Average follow-up was 8 years. Lower mortality rates were seen for the higher fitness categories. Optimal fitness levels were seen at 9 METs for women and 10 METs for men. Attributable risk estimates for all-cause mortality indicated that a low fitness level was an important risk factor in both men and women.

FUEL YOUR METABOLISM

Quality nutrition is key to supporting your exercise efforts and boosting your metabolism. Build your meals with a quality protein base (20-30gm of protein) and add a quality carbohydrate (such as vegetables) and a healthy fat. Your snacks should be based the same with the protein amount 6-10gm of protein. Avoid eating carbohydrates by themselves. This can spike your blood sugar, which contributes to increase in visceral fat. When grabbing fruit add a protein and healthy fat. A handful of seeds or nuts is a great pairing, or top fruit with high protein granola.

Fuel your efforts with the nutrition trifecta… protein, quality carb and healthy fat!

STUFFED JALAPEÑOS WITH GOAT
CHEESE & PANCETTA

These jalapeno bites are a great metabolism boosting snack. Jalapenos are a good source of vitamins A & C. They have the active compound called capsaicin, which gives peppers their heat. Recent research suggests this compound can boost your metabolism. Goat cheese is lower in calories than most cheeses and is a good source of vitamin A and K, calcium and protein. Pancetta is not smoked as most bacon, it has 9 gm of protein per 2 oz. 2 of these is approximately 38 calories and 6gm of protein.

Infused waters can be great to assist in hydration. Infused water with lemon, ginger and mint gives a powerful health boost. It improves digestion, fights heartburn, soothes the stomach and has powerful anti-inflammatory and antioxidant properties. Deliciously refreshing.

Workout smarter not harder with Metabolic Makeover Workouts. Improve your health and fitness by increasing your VO2 and boosting your metabolism.

CARDIOZONE® makes it as easy as 1,2,3.